W9-BAH-629

For Mike and Margaret

Joy! Love! Light!

Donna P. Savage
2009

The Man and The Shark
Donna P. Savage

Photography
by Daryl A. Pritchard

THE MAN AND THE SHARK, A Modern Day Fable of Awakening and Rebirth, Copyright©2008 by Donna P. Savage. All rights reserved. No part of this book may be used or reproduced in any manner whatsoever without written permission from the author, except in the case of brief quotations embodied in critical articles and reviews. Published in the United States by Canzada & Company Publishing, 64 Island Drive S., Friday Harbor, Washington 98250.

Copyright permission for photos obtained from Daryl A. Pritchard, and for artwork from Debbie Martin.

To purchase a copy of this book, photos or artwork, please contact Donna P. Savage via email to donnapsavage@live.com or visit online at www.donnapsavage.com.

ISBN 978-0-9821582-0-3 Library of Congress Pending. Printed in Korea.

Publisher's Note: The scanning, uploading, and distribution of this work via the Internet or via any other means without the permission of the publisher is illegal and punishable by law. Please purchase only authorized electronic editions, and do not participate in or encourage electronic piracy of copyrighted materials. Your support of the author's rights is appreciated.

My deepest gratitude to my parents, Charles and Marie Pritchard, for the many levels of support you provided during the completion of this book—you made it easy for me to work. My thanks also goes to Howard Cain, Susan Gerle, Susan Garrett, and Dan Grippo for insights into the story; Susan Key and Tom Pulley for their initial editing; and the Puerto Vallarta and Kingston Writer's Groups, valuable forums for the work in process. A special thanks goes to my mother for her extensive editing and daily feedback. Finally, thank you to my brother Daryl Pritchard for his dedication to the completion of this work—and whose photography was the inspiration for the story.

Donna P. Savage

I dedicate this book to the boy who can fly.

The Man and The Shark

Not so long ago, a boy was born into this world believing. He remembered where he came from before he was born, and knew that he was a glorious being.

Until the age of three, he recalled distinctly his last home, a splendid city, surrounded in fluid, swirling colors that he moved through like water, requiring no oxygen to breathe.

There his soul had thrived— abundant, joyful, and free, preparing him for his time on earth.

Intrigued with this new world, the boy's curious spirit led him on an experimental journey.

Willful, he climbed out of his playpen and crib—he would not be confined, and cried if his parents hindered him.

He put milkshake in a steam iron and tumble-dried a wet cat. He took apart the radio, the camera and the clock. He tasted crayons, ants, ammonia, and chalk.

He tested everything, including his mother's patience.

The boy attempted to fly, his inspiration fueled by vague memories of his previous home when he moved easily any direction he chose.

Many times he spread his arms and jumped off the garden wall, always landing hard on the ground, the wind knocked out of him.

After a particularly rough landing, he mused, "It is true. I cannot fly. After all, I am only a boy."

7

One day, the boy was running fast down a hill. He felt the wind rush against his chest and he leaned into it. In that instant, his feet no longer touched the ground. He was barely two feet aloft but he was flying! From that day on, the boy flew often and found it easiest in his dreams.

One night he flew to his favorite place, the seashore. A whale shark swimming near the ocean's surface spied the boy hovering two feet above the shoreline. The shark exclaimed, "I did not know that man can fly!" He was so curious that he swam close to the shore and as the tide ebbed, was beached upon the sand. Still able to breathe, the astonished shark stood up using his tail, lifted his fin and called out to the boy, "Comrade, fly over here!"

The boy did. The boy and the shark were amazed to find that they understood each other. They communicated through their hearts, creating resonance that registered in their inner vision as pictures and in their bodies as feelings, and all was clear between them. They discovered that they were old friends, having lived in the city of swirling colors when their bodies were shapes of celestial light.

The birds of the sky and other fish of the sea observed the boy and the shark conversing on the beach. This excited them, and they moved closer to see what it was all about. By the end of the day, the boy talked to every fish and every bird, and they recognized each other as kin, unified as beings of the world in different forms.

On that day, the whale shark and the boy made a pact. They pledged abiding friendship, to always trust each other, to meet often in the boy's dreams, and someday upon the earth.

Shortly thereafter, the boy and his parents went to the zoo. He carried his first camera along, excited and eager to use it. At the white tiger's cage, the boy was so enthralled that he felt he would burst from the love pouring from his heart to the tiger.

In response, the tiger surprised the boy by rolling over on its back and looking at him humorously. Within seconds, the tiger sent images into the boy's heart and feelings into his body, just as the fish and the birds had, and the boy understood the tiger perfectly.

That day he realized that he could communicate with all beings of the earth.

He understood that what he envisioned was real—what he felt inside was real. He saw that life on earth offered experiences of unity and blending similar to those of his prior life.

Soon however, he noticed that no one else talked to animals or birds or fish. No one else could fly.

When he spoke of these things, people laughed at him, patted his head, and said, "You are a very imaginative boy!" Their teasing made him feel ill at ease so he quit speaking of what he knew.

The boy saw into people just like other beings, noting that their words and actions belied the messages of their hearts. Communication with them was like jumping off the garden wall, only more painful and to little avail.

The boy took refuge in his inner life, shutting out a world that troubled and bemused him.

With headphones on the boy closed himself off and tuned his ears to the music of his soul. Thus cocooned, he spent hours writing poetry or creating imagery from his photos.

Often he drifted into a dream state, traveling to his home faraway where he was open and free.

The boy matured, adapting to the outer world by responding rationally to others, heeding only their words and ignoring the messages he perceived from their hearts.

This practice made life with people more manageable, yet added to a growing sadness in his soul.

He soon set aside all memories of the boy who can fly, burying all that did not fit in the "real" world.

By the time the boy had grown into a man, his ability to see into the hearts of all beings had been relegated to his dreams—dreams that, as a man, he could no longer recall.

Today, the man is a realist who works at a practical job requiring linear thought and no nonsense. It devours his time and his marrow, his creativity consigned to hobbies.

Both photographer and diver, the man indulges his lifelong passion for the ocean every year. For twenty years, he has allotted one week of his vacation time to its depths, swimming among its beings, camera in hand.

He envies their freedom to move easily through the expansive underwater world. As he swims among them, he feels a similar freedom, and senses what it might be like to fly, moving any direction on a whim.

When he frolics with dolphins, time stands still. These carefree moments take him back to childhood, evoking joyful memories otherwise lost to him. He imagines sharing these memories with the dolphins by sending them images that flash from his heart.

Back on dry land, the man discards his wetsuit along with his fantasies. He dons his logical facade and chastises himself for pretending the dolphins understand him. "It is impossible. I am only a man."

What he thinks does not reflect what he feels. His reality is that during those 7 days each year, 140 days over 20 years, the man is most alive, his life force revitalized.

His heart expands during those brief periods, fueled by sensations from the time when he was one with all beings.

You see, the man no longer knows who he is or from where he came. Still, the beings of the earth know. The boy who can fly knows.

The man remembers nothing. The man would have laughed at the boy and his vivid imagination, just as other adults had done. Yet his favorite T-shirts depict the lost city of Atlantis, an imaginary city that exists in another space in time.

The man does not know that imagination is real.

Away from the sea, the man's life is barren. He lives in the middle of a vast, arid land, foreign to his natural state of being.

He does not relate his sense of emptiness to the absence of the ocean holding him in its embrace. Yet when he bought a house, he chose one located on Ocean Drive.

The synchronicity of his choice was lost on the man. He thought, simply, that he chose this house because he liked it best.

The man decorated his home with treasures he collected over the years. Only one living room wall remains bare because no picture seems to fit there.

Otherwise, his mantle is cluttered with figurines of dolphins and his walls a collection of prints of the wild— eagles that soar high above the earth, and big cats that roam the plains.

These are his kin, but he does not regard them in that way.

Looking upon their images makes him happy, and inspires him to create images of his own.

When he photographs animals he talks to them, doing his best to imitate their sounds, pretending they understand him.

He is patient, and has often sat for hours outside a burrow, waiting for a rabbit or a prairie dog to become at ease with him and pop out of its hole to pose for his ready camera.

The man never questions his natural affinity with animals. He is grateful, in his quiet way, for their company, and treats them with gentleness and respect.

The animals, in turn, recognize him as a familiar, and allow him brief passage into their worlds.

The man visits zoos and wildlife preserves to see his favorite subjects, the big cats.

Each visit increases his awareness of the negative impact of confinement on their lives. It makes him uncomfortable. To compensate, he creates an illusion of freedom by eliminating their cages, when possible, from his photos.

On one occasion when he successfully renders an image of a tiger in what appears to be its natural habitat, he notices a tightening in his gut, and a wave of nausea passes over him.

He identifies with the illusion. It is as if—he too, is living in a cage, only his is truly invisible, and held there by an inexplicable force.

His cage is his mundane life. He moves on a lackluster circuit between his home and his work, losing life force over the years as his enthusiasm gradually drains from him.

His days, nights and weekends are spent in cyberspace.

The computer is central to his job, it is his source of entertainment, and it is his way of connecting with people, especially women.

In his youth, the man loved
from a distance, holding
those he coveted within the
frame of his camera lens,
but rarely in his arms.

Relationships he desires
are like shadows—when he
reaches out, they are always
beyond his grasp.

So, he loves from afar,
his mind having created a
chasm he cannot cross.

He is very lonely and
understands not how this
came to be. He yearns to
be touched.

He wants, very much, to
love and be loved.

To compensate for his loneliness, the man develops relationships remotely through his computer, his fingertips caressing a keypad. From a distance, he expresses his deepest feelings, his wildest dreams, and his most passionate desires.

He creates an illusion of love in cyberspace, a place where he is safe from pain, his heart ensconced in his poetry and beautiful words.

Many years have passed in this comfort zone—familiar though disheartening, and it has become the norm for the man.

He has learned to detach from his emotions, monitoring them as he would his favorite website. His mind has created a special file marked "Inaccessible" into which he places all that he is no longer willing to acknowledge.

On the rare occasion when the man's emotions do surface, they overwhelm him.

His own depths frighten him.

Rather than be lost in that raging sea, the man thinks of a rational explanation for his feelings and files them away.

The man often distracts himself by eating when he is bored, frustrated, sad, or angry.

He consumes foods void of nutrition, packed with sugar and artificial stimulants. The stimulants activate his thoughts, diverting his emotions. The empty foods feed his immediate hunger needs, but do not satiate the lingering hunger of his spirit.

His essence is hidden within the recesses of his body, camouflaging his personality as well as his pain.

He feels very little. He believes in very little.

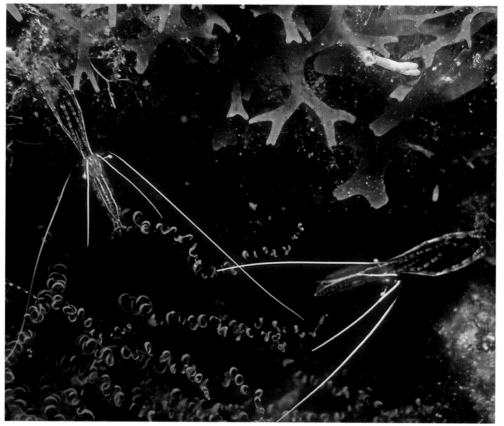

The man believes only in what he can see and touch and is skeptical of people who speak of God or "All That Is." He does not see himself as part of the whole, the One, inseparable from all beings and the entire universe.

He does not believe in miracles. He does not believe in things intangible, and has little patience for stories and fantasies of unknown worlds.

Yet his pictures capture the essence of those worlds and the miracle of all creation.

Immersed in the ocean, the man experiences great joy and love for all beings. Each is flawless in his eyes, from the miniscule to the giant, and when faced with the formidable ones, he is fearless.

Most beings of the sea ignore the man. When they look his direction, they perceive another of their kin and see no reason to stop and chat since they are busy on their way.

Others, with a wider view of the world, often speak to him in their own language, telling him stories, guiding him along.

One day, an old whale shark is excited to see his friend, recognizing him as the boy who can fly. The shark is delighted that their agreement to meet has manifested. He jokes playfully with the man who can no longer fly and who swims with a snorkel in his mouth and flippers on his feet. The shark teases the man because he is gill-less.

The shark enjoys seeing his kin in this new form and envies his freedom of movement in the foreign not-wet world. The old shark heard about the man's world from lucky fish that told tales of surviving hapless visits there. The shark believes this other world that he cannot see or touch is real, although he has no experience of it himself. He questions the man about his grand adventure in the strange other world outside the water, a world beyond the shark's comprehension.

The shark soon realizes that the man is oblivious to his musings and teasing. He then makes a greater effort to connect with the man by flooding him with images from his heart, reminding him that this is the manner in which they communicate. He transmits their many visits in dreams and their agreement to meet upon the earth. Finally, the shark stops, accepting that his efforts are in vain. He promises the man, "Comrade, we will meet again. Call to me when you are ready and I will come to you!'

The man hears nothing. After all, he no longer believes that beings can speak, and he has long since forgotten his dreams. Still, he responds to the old shark, swimming alongside him contentedly, more at ease than ever before.

During that outstanding afternoon, the man is filled with joy as he experiences oneness with the shark and other underwater beings. Yet he has no words to speak this truth out loud.

Soon after, an artist gives the man an abstract triptych in exchange for photographing her work. The triptych is unlike anything she has ever created, her inspiration a mystery to her. She senses that the paintings hold special meaning for the man. When he sees the paintings, tears leap into his eyes. "They are extraordinary," he utters, barely able to express his thanks as emotions surge through him. He leaves quickly, compelled to take the paintings home.

When he arrives on Ocean Drive, he goes straight to his living room and hangs the triptych on the vacant wall. He stands there, staring at the paintings, soaking in their magic—when suddenly his knees buckle under him as he feels a place within himself open, and from it emerges an overwhelming mix of joy and love and deep, deep sorrow.

The abstract paintings depict the home of his soul, a home visible only to him. There in the largest painting lives the glorious lifetime of the man before he was a boy, before he was born into this world. Unbeknownst to the artist, she painted within a universe a city that floats in swirling, fluid colors. In these luminous colors the man's soul thrives, moving through them as a fish through water.

Foreign yet familiar impressions flood him. The paintings portray places and beings he knows, all bodies of celestial light shaped in vague forms. As the man sinks into the images, he feels the sensation of swirling colors moving through him and around him. He no longer has skin, but only a thin membrane that defines his body. He feels no separation between himself and all that he holds as beloved. As he moves amongst the other beings, his body remembers the tremendous joy of his life with them. With each he senses their abiding love and acceptance of him. One being in particular resonates with him as the whale shark of his dreams, and he recognizes his timeless friend with great joy!

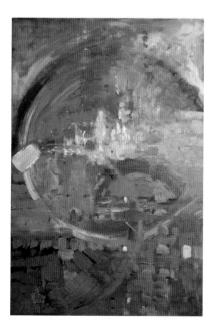

Abruptly, his ecstasy is torn from him and he is transported to the moment of his birth when he left his soul's home behind.

Dumbfounded by the sudden shift in realities, the man feels claustrophobic within his own skin as he collapses on the floor. He curls into fetal position and sobs, feeling his loss of connection, his separation—the sacrifice he made to be born.

His agonized mind screams for control. "What is happening to me? This can't be real!"

His experience stretches beyond the boundaries of his beliefs. He cannot frame it. It fits no structure that he knows.

Nevertheless, since that day of his awakening, the man is changed.

He feels unsettled as he tries to make his life work for him, now acutely aware that it is foreign to his nature. He is caught—trapped, just like his favorite felines in the zoo.

He does not see that his invisible cage is his own creation, his confinement born from his choices to close off feelings that make his heart soar.

The man places no meaning in metaphor, synchronicity, or coincidence. He prays to nothing, conforms to no dogma, and follows no spiritual path. Still, he is keenly aware of a voice within, calling him home.

The voice within is the source of all his joy.

It is up to the man to heed that voice and align his life with his beckoning spirit.

He may resist moving beyond his cage, making changes that feed his yearning, hungering soul—yet there is no turning back.

Whether or not he "believes," his inner voice is guiding him to acknowledge all that he knows.

He knows what it is to swim among the sharks, gliding along as their brethren.

He knows what it is to face a ferocious moray eel, bursting from its cave.

He knows what it is to touch the skin of whale sharks and dolphins, just as he would a dear friend.

He knows the joys of communion with all beings of the sea, even though their voices are mute to him just as his own voice has been.

He knows that the world in which he spends the majority of his days seems senseless and lifeless when he views it from the perspective of the sea, the place so closely resembling his true home.

The man knows aloneness and separation as his closest companions.

Now is the time for the man to tap into his power, his source, to go into the place that is as deep as the sea, to feel his emotions, and set himself free.

Only he can do this, but his mind has yet to comprehend the connection between his suppressed feelings and his suppressed life.

He wants to change his life, and he calls out in his dreams at night—

"Help me to see! Believe in me!"

The whale shark hears the summons from the depths of the sea. He enters the man's dream, keeping his commitment to him.

The shark has believed in the man even when the man did not believe. Now the shark will stand by the man during this reckoning with his soul, ready to nudge him into a new life.

The man is floating on the ocean when he sees his friend surface from below. He greets the whale shark, asking, "Why are you here?"

The old shark speaks to him in their shared language, saying, "So you can remember."

At the shark's words, the ocean shapes itself into a mirror, and reflected therein is the boy who can fly. The shark says to the man, "Now is the time to recall your story. Listen. Watch."

The man looks into the mirror at the boy who can fly, and the boy says to him—

"There is so much I want to tell you then maybe you will remember!... At one time, you and I were one.... You left me behind because I did not want to be sad with you.... I once lived in the city of swirling colors but now I live on earth.... I have loads of fun here!... My favorite thing is to fly two feet above the ground!... It feels a lot like how I moved in the city of swirling colors!... One time I flew to the seashore and that is when I met the whale shark ... we knew each other from the city of swirling colors.... I learned that I can talk with my heart ... the way I am talking to you now.... I send pictures and feelings from it into you!... The day I talked to the shark I talked to fish and birds too!... They understood everything I said!... I also go to the zoo and talk to animals there ... the white tiger was the first.... He is my friend!"

"I can talk to people through their hearts too ... but they don't like it ... they tease me to hide how they feel.... They shut me out!

I stopped talking to them because I had to try too hard and then I could not sense other beings ... not bird or fish or sky or tiger or grass or tree. I wanted to feel good so I had to let people be!

I knew this meant that I would remain fixed in time, and you would forget I ever existed—unless this day of remembering happened, and for that, there was no guarantee. The only time you connected with me was when you were swimming in the sea—you felt me then, and a few times when you photographed the big cats."

As the boy talks, the man looks deep into his eyes until he is lost in them, and the boy's memories become his own, the boy's voice also his own, the boy's body his own.

The memories flood forth and the man's feelings erupt with them, welling up in great waves. He flounders as wave upon wave crashes upon him, dragging him under with their power, releasing him for an instant, then dragging him deeper.

He loses sight of the boy who can fly. The man is terrified as his own depths swallow him. He struggles. He fights. He is drowning. His life is ending. He is consumed in grief for all that he has not lived.

He calls out desperately, "PLEASE HELP ME!" as he gasps his last breath.

The whale shark moves underneath him, buoying him up in the currents long enough for the man to catch his breath. That is when the man senses the shark's voice inside his heart, "Your emotions are the key to your treasured, hidden life. Do not resist. Dive deeper."

The man implicitly trusts the familiar voice known to the boy who can fly. He gives up his struggle and dives into the darkest recesses of his soul, knowing that no matter how dark the darkness, the shark is watching over him.

In the depths, the mirror then plays back his entire life to him—a video on fast reverse revealing his choices and all the pain, anger, and isolation long buried.

In its reflection, the man sees at his side a shadow, and therein enumerated are the companions that stood patiently beside his loneliness, awaiting his acknowledgment.

He witnesses himself heedless of those who are ready to love him throughout his life, his heart obscured by childhood disillusionment and sadness.

He sees himself focusing on his separation, making his choices, and building his cage.

He cries out in anguish as he recognizes himself as his own captor.

Then the man beholds for the first time—the miracles he has experienced and catalogued through his camera lens all along, and he sees the divinity in each being.

He hears
cheers in the
background, a
symphony of
voices, rejoicing
at his courage
to look at his
life.

His illusion of
separation is
shattered. He
feels the truth
that he is not
alone.

With this
revelation, his
joy cascades
over him in one
great wave, and
his old life is
washed away.

He surfaces from the depths, his heart pulsing, his blood racing, his body floating, his spirit soaring, and he flies into the clouds to join his eagle kin.

Free from the entanglement of his past, he accepts the eagle's gifts of liberty and broad vision.

He visualizes a new life.

The beings of the earth join in to lend him their strength, playfulness and instinct.

Sensing them, the man is imbued with these same qualities, and recognizes their guidance as his own.

He suddenly knows all that he has always known since the time before he was born.

He is one with the sea and land and sky!

A strange and wonderful new feeling floods over him. Reflected in his face is a glow of gratitude for his entire life, all his joys and all his pain that brought him to this moment now.

He reaches into the mirror and draws out the boy who can fly, embraces him, and takes his hand.

He says to the boy, "From now on, we are one. I promise to cherish and protect you and love you. I will never abandon you again!"

He then makes peace with himself, accepting responsibility for all that he has created and all that he will now create.

Now the man walks down the street,
a light glowing and shining from him,
his eyes bright, his countenance joyful,
his step light.

He looks straight into the eyes of each
person he meets, straight into their
hearts. He fills them with his joy and
his love.

They respond to him without words.
They open their light to him just as
they receive his light. They recognize
the man as their kin.

The man walks on by—and
all are enriched by this silent
communication, this silent exchange.

This feeling of oneness radiates from within each person, empowering all beings in their world. The beings in the man's world are likewise empowered by his prevailing light, and unity of consciousness expands with every encounter.

This takes place and requires no exchange of words, no agreement of minds, and no one to believe in anything they choose not to believe.

AND SO IT IS.

Donna Savage is an adventurer on the inner and outer planes, a traveler and a writer, drawing her inspiration from the beauty of people and places she inhabits.

This book was conceived during a time when the author was resisting the steady voice within, thus creating havoc in her life. It was completed as she once again awakened, her inner voice leading her in a new direction, and into a life dedicated to joyous living.

She divides her time between San Juan Island, Washington, East Tennessee, and Puerto Vallarta, Mexico, all homes in her heart.

To arrange book signings or presentations, contact Donna via email at **donnapsavage@live.com** or for more information, visit her website, **www.donnapsavage.com**.

Daryl Ambress Pritchard is a photographer and scuba diver who enjoys capturing images of his favorite animals above and below the water's surface, connecting with them through the lens of his camera. Some, like Paco shown here become his friends. He favors the Caribbean for his scuba diving and proudly says the Fort Worth Zoo is one of the jewels in his home state of Texas. Many of his photographs are shared online at **www.ambress.com** and may be purchased upon an inquiry by email to **daryl@ambress.com**.

Reader Preview Endorsements

"Ms. Savage describes her work as "a modern fable." It is that and more. She traces the age-old story of the loss of innocence that everyone undergoes in becoming an adult, and its recovery beyond the tragedy of self-alienation—through art, nature, and recollection. She does this without resorting at any point to religious or philosophical language. It is a fine accomplishment, an aid to meditation at the very least, and at most a way "home" for the wandering soul." Don Morris, Minister, Kingston TN

"This succinct, delightful book packs a powerful message, and the photographs add dimension to the different elements of the story. I have read it many times. It's a keeper!" Lana Dahl, CranioSacral Therapist, Seattle, WA

"This is an uplifting and inspirational book, full of insights that anyone can use to improve and refocus their life. It is a reminder of the important things in life—love, connection and gratitude." Laurel George, Advertising Consultant, Atlanta GA

"This delightful book reminds me to live my passion—and that makes me a better mother by example. My 4-year old son is too young to understand most of the text but he loves the pictures and asks me to read the story about the man who talks to animals." H.W. Ernst, Architect/High Performance Auto Driver, Denver CO

"Donna has masterfully woven a simple yet profound tale of how the future will be won, not by learning who we are, but by remembering who we are." Hugh Gilbert, KCTpl IOGT, Author and International Lecturer, Calgary, Alberta Canada